Obsidian Blades:

Decolonizing Poetry for the Liberation of Indigenous People in Occupied Amerikkka

Citlalli Citlalmina Anahuac

Print Version 6/10/14

Graphics and photography by:

Olin Tezcatlipoca
Carlos Cordova
Ruben Castro
Ocelotl Cuitlahuac
Taizet Hernandez
Citlalli C. Anahuac
Arlene Valdez Pinedo

Art by Nelyollotl Toltecatl

Dedication:

Dedicated to all of the warrior women of the western hemisphere whose names we will never know.

Dedicated to all of my sisters and brothers who are under attack by white supremacy. We are a beautiful people and little by little we will decolonize ourselves and rebuild ourselves as the creative and amazing world force we once were.

Dedicated to my life long teacher, tlamatini, mentor, and friend Olin Tezcatlipoca, founder and director of the Mexica Movement (www.mexica-movement.org). Thank you for 17 years of guidance, discipline, and support.

Dedicated to all the members and supporters of the Mexica Movement. Each one of you inspire me and help me continue on this path for true liberation.

Dedicated to the 100 million of our ancestors that were killed by the European genocidal machine since 1492.

Every day of life is a new opportunity to change
to resist
to create
to break free
from the bullshit that drowns your potential

AWOAPUMA COLOQUE
OF
TAWANTINSUYU NATION
ICAN TLACA CONFEDERATION

NICAN TLACA WARRIORS
EDUCATION FOR LIBERATION

CITLALLI ANAHUAC
OF
MEXICA MOVEMENT
NICAN TLACA CONFEDERATIO

Pledge of Resistance
(Collective poem read with our youth)

I am an original inhabitant of this land
I am not an illegal alien
I am not a foreigner on my own land
I am Nican Tlaca
I am Indigenous
I am beautiful
I am brown
I am light brown
I am dark brown
I am beautiful
I have the right to be free

I have the right to be me
I have the right to walk anywhere on my continent
I love you
I love me
We are all one people
This is our land
We will be free!

2008

*I love to read this collective poem before I share my poetry. Here is a sample of it in full life:

http://www.youtube.com/watch?v=hh4kgu3FlK8
http://www.youtube.com/watch?v=1QA85JehbOw

WE ARE NOT HISPANIC OR LATINO

By grouping all people who speak Spanish into one category, corporations can target one audience at the same time and therefore maximize exposure and profit. They don't care about proper representation and cultural identity. It's a colonial power tool to keep us as ignorant fools.

We are not Hispanic or Latino
Those terms do not define our people
speaking the language doesn't make you the ethnicity
Grouping us all together is a marketing scheme
they want to kill us with white supremacy

We are not Hispanic or Latino
We refuse to identify with colonial terms
Defining Europeans by killing the Indigenous
The time has now come to put an end to this

Colonizers hold the power of definition
They want us to exist as slaves ad give no recognition
To our ownership of our land and its total restitution
By taking away our names, we are bound to mental chains
Ignorant of our ancient history till we end up in our graves

We are not Hispanic or Latino
Those terms do not define our people
speaking the language doesn't make you the ethnicity
Grouping us all together is a marketing scheme
they want to kill us with white supremacy

Since 1492 our lands and our identity
Have been victim of the hands of white supremacy
Stripping us of our true connection to our history
Its time we end to this colonial legacy

We are not Hispanic or Latino
Those terms do not define our people
speaking the language doesn't make you the ethnicity
Grouping us all together is a marketing scheme
they want to kill us with white supremacy

We are Indigenous people killed ethnically
Mislabeled and branded as a herd of sheep
We are kept ignorant and culturally asleep
Being raped and terrorized for 5 centuries
Kept ignorant of what really happened
The genocide of our people is quickly forgotten

We are not Hispanic or Latino
Those terms do not define our people
speaking the language doesn't make you the ethnicity
Grouping us all together is a marketing scheme
they want to kill us with white supremacy

we were forbidden to speak our languages
we are blind to see all of the colonial damages
Branding us like slaves, slaving us in fatal caves
Plucking our original names
And now we falsely claim
The Spanish royal lineage?

Spain is not our motherland
Its another lie created to keep us in self-hate
We must liberate our minds and begin to understand
we must resist to the colonial traps they create
They continue to benefit and we don't have a clue
Don't let Univision, TV Azteca and telemundo fool you
Europeans speaking Spanish don't speak for you and me
Simply speaking Spanish doesn't make us the ethnicity
Grouping us all together is just a marketing scheme
A way to make us all buy their products by making us believe
That we are identical and we all have the same needs
Maximizing profits targeting only one audience
What a great marketing monopoly
They save money
And we lose our identity

We are not Hispanic or Latino
Those terms do not define our people
speaking the language doesn't make you the ethnicity
Grouping us all together is a marketing scheme
they want to kill us with white supremacy

We are not from Europe
Not Italians, Romans, French, Portuguese
We are not the children of Columbus or Cortez
Speaking English doesn't make Black people British
Speaking Spanish doesn't make a Chinese Hispanic
There is no logic to this if you take time to think about it
Apply the same reasoning to other communities
Soon you will see the colonial representations
It's a false colonial fraudulent unity

Spanish speaking Europeans still dominate our governments
Our education systems and our resources
There has never been true independence
Just European civil wars on our continent
Whether they speak Spanish or English
European settlers are still in power
We are not Hispanic or Latino
Those terms do not define our people
speaking the language doesn't make you the ethnicity
Grouping us all together is a marketing scheme
they want to kill us with white supremacy

It's not that we are a melting pot
We are being cooked alive

It's not that we are a melting pot
We are being cooked alive

We are not Hispanic or Latino
Those terms do not define our people
speaking the language doesn't make you the ethnicity
Grouping us all together is a marketing scheme
they want to kill us with white supremacy

2013

Watch my video version of this poem:
http://www.youtube.com/watch?v=FRTZAGisiDg

9

Gran Marcha 3/28/2009

Ode to Malcolm X by an Indigenous Woman
PUBLIC DISCLAIMER:

Dear Malcolm X,
I want to share my deep admiration and respect with these words.
Every time I hear you speak, you speak to me. You speak to Mexicans, Central
Americans, Native Americans, and South Americans but most of us are ignorant of the
connection.
So if I may, I'd like to borrow your words and passion and dedicate them to my people.
We are in great need of clarity and an assertive view of who we are.
Thank you for being a warrior for justice and a warrior for your people.

Who are you?
You don't know!
Don't tell me Hispanic and latino?

10

What were you before the white man called you Hispanic and latino? Raza and mestizo?
And where were you?
You were here on this continent
And what did you have?
What was yours?
What language did you speak?
What was your name?
It could not have been *Hernandez, Garcia, Vasquez*
They don't have those names where you and I come from
NO!
What was YOUR name
And why don't you know what your name was then?
Where did it go?
When did you lose it?
Where did you lose it?
Who took it?
And how did they take it?
What tongue did you speak and how did the man take your tongue?
Where is your history?
And how did the man wipe out your history?
Who taught you to hate the color of your skin?
Who taught you to hate the color of your hair?
Who taught you to hate the shape of your nose and the shape of your lips?
Who taught you to hate yourself from the top of your head to the soles of your feet?
Who taught you to hate your own kind?
Who taught you to hate the race that you belong to so much so that you don't want to
be around each other?
Who taught you to kill yourselves, brown on brown
Who taught us that the word Mexican/Central American/Native American/South
American was dirty and to avoid its use at all instances
Who taught us to accept this shit
Who taught us to stop fighting
Who taught us to pledge allegiance to a colonial country
Who taught us that theft was o.k
that genocide is normal
Who taught you to call yourself Hispanic and latino
Who taught you how to stay ignorant
Who taught us to ask if our babies are born light
does the baby have blue eyes
Who taught you that only white is beautiful
Who taught you to sellout
Who taught you to forget about your history
500 years have taught us well.
500 years of genocide

Indian schools taught us that
Their swords taught us that
Their lies written and distributed in Europe taught us that
Our schools teach us that
Modern day Indian schools
they've injected lies
slaves are ignorant
lies keep slaves slaves
slaves keep lies alive
tell the slave he has no brain
he won't bother using it
tell the slave that he is free
and that those chains are bracelets
tell the slave he should be lucky to eat at the masters table
tell him to be thankful you own him cus what we he do without you
lies for slaves
lies uncovered
dead we lay in graves
still in ignorance
and still we think we're free
and never question our own identity
You see Malcolm you talked about embracing ourselves.
That we need cultural spines, we need to be fearless when reclaiming our heritage,
history, and identity.
You taught us about being UNAPOLOGETIC FOR BEING who we are!
You taught us not to forget about the crimes against us!
You taught that to Africans/Blacks
But the shoe fits us too
The shoe fits us all
And I am gonna wear it
We will never forget what happened to us in 1492.
But how do we fight to not forget something that we don't even know
Our history is a mystery
There's dots but we can't connect them
There's blood but we don't know where its coming from
There's pain but we don't know what to do make it go away
But we're learning
We're learning that we survived the bloodiest years in humanity's history
we're learning what genocide means
we're learning what courage means
we're learning self-pride
we're learning that being light skinned only means that we have deeper racial rape
scars
and that it will never take us away from being FULLY INDIGENOUS!

We are learning our history
As Indigenous, not mestizo
Not half of anything
But fully Indigenous, Nican Tlaca
And as we learn
We get angry
We realize the depth of this oppression
We realize the true definition of colonization
We are getting angry cus we're beginning to feel the fire of racism
We're sick of Disney and their nazi Mcintyre
We're sick of white supremacists being hosts through the wire
We are gonna burn down the masters house
And rebuild ourselves
The time will always be now
People just started asking how
Like the Mapuche in the Andes
We will never give up our lands
Like Zapata and Villa
Land and liberation
That is our commitment
Let's take up this generation
Today and every day until liberation will be the day of resistance.
The day to say no to the continuing genocide
Genocide cus we are living without millions of our people by our side
Cus they killed over 100 million of us
And they think that we're too many
Genocide because our identity is butchered everyday
Genocide because our history is a mystery
Genocide because we don't even know that we are victims of genocide where 95% of
our population was killed. Genocide.
Genocide: because we don't know our true culture
Genocide: because we lack knowledge of who we were, who we are, and who we
should be
Genocide: because we no longer speak in the language of our people. We speak like
fake white people. Spanish or English.
But it is hard for many Mexicans, Central Americans, Native Americans, South
Americans to grasp these words cus we are so brainwashed with the mestizo bullshit.
We are not half white people, we are not half Europeans.
We are full-blooded and mixed-blooded Indigenous people.
The last 500 years ain't shit compared to our ancient history
We are sick and tired and lies being told to us sometimes by our professors, parents,
loved ones.
We are getting sick
We vomit

lies, all the self-hate that your lies generate, we are sick and we are tired.
Sedated with money and luxury, sedated with gangs and material shit, sedated and
integrated into the matrix of white supremacy,
Usually when people are sad, they don't do anything. They just cry over their condition.
But when they get angry, they bring about a change.
Yeah its sad to see our people dying
Ignorant and ashamed of their heritage,
Yes it is sad.
But it makes me mad because it is Anger
Anger
Angry
Righteously so
Change
Cus we don't like what is going on
We are tired of being called illegal on our own land
Cus we are tired of being on our knees
Begging for acceptance into a society that feeds off of our sweat
And we're tired of being told to feel lucky
That we are here
The best place in the world
but
"I'm not going to sit at your table and watch you eat, with nothing on my plate, and call
myself a diner. Sitting at the table doesn't make you a diner, unless you eat some of
what's on that plate. Being here in America doesn't make you an American.... No I'm
not an American. I'm one of the millions of Mexicans, Central Americans, Native
Americans, South Americans, NICAN TLACA people who are the victims of
Americanism.... I'm speaking as a victim of this American system. And I see America
through the eyes of a victim. I don't see any American dream; I see an American
nightmare."
I see drugs
Alcohol
Our youth killing each other on the streets
I see violence
I see teenage pregnancies
I see parents who are too tired to rock their own babies to sleep
I see generations lost in addictions
I see beautiful women locked into low-self-esteem
I see beautiful men drown in their drinks
I see America for what it really is
A nightmare
But the problem is that we are not asleep
"If we don't stand for something, we may fall for anything."
Fall for street name
Fall for a love game

14

Fall for a million bucks
Fall for that liquid that numbs your veins
Fall for short term solutions that hide away the pain
We have to stand for our land
Stand for our land
And fall to nothing
Not again
We're just getting up
From the fall
The fall of our cities
The fall of our accomplishments
The fall of our pride
The fall that has lasted more than 500 years
Get up and dust away
Clean yourself of filth
"We're not Americans, we're Nican Tlaca! (MEXICANS, CENTRAL AMERICANS, NATIVE
AMERICANS, SOUTH AMERICANS) who happen to be on our own land
We are Nican Tlaca
We did not get here on a boat in 1492
We did not come from Europe
Europe came here
Europe came to us
"We declare our right on this *continent* to be *Nican Tlaca* to be respected as so, to be
given the rights of a human being in this society, on this earth, in this day, which we
intend to bring into existence *by any means necessary*."
By any means necessary
But we must start with knowledge
To know is to grow
To grow in courage
Grow in dedication
To know is to be armed with the power of truth
By any means necessary
We are tired of colonialism
We want to call ourselves by the names we called each other
We want to speak like we spoke
We want our lands back
You know the whole continent that you stole
Remember the marches
The protests
The walkouts
The word is getting out
My people are developing courage
My people are getting angry
My people are awakening

And you what about you?
Are you asleep?
Asleep like we used to be?
Dreaming of America
While they dig us deep
But I don't mean to depress you
I don't mean to impress you
I do mean to make you see
See the beauty that knowledge and truth will bring
I do mean to shake you up and possibly inspire you to speak
To speak in the defense of our people
To act in the defense of our people
Cus if you don't do it
No one else will
I am not sure who else can
You see,
We're young and strong
Brown, educated, and infuriated,
And with all the right
To be pisst off at such violent injustice
There will be nothing holding us back
500 years is far too long
Nobody can give you freedom. Nobody can give you equality or justice or anything. If you're a man and woman, you take it.

2009

Watch my video version of this poem:
http://www.youtube.com/watch?v=JQc-kjlS5UE

Chichen Itza 7/2011

18

The War Cry of The forgotten women:

See these Obsidian blades shoot out my mouth
Show you the rage of a people locked in a cage
Built with their bones and fed their own blood
Hear our war cry, we the forgotten women,
See these Obsidian blades shoot out my mouth
Our presence rejected on the white man's page
See these Obsidian blades shoot out my mouth
As I tell you now the story of us
Clear all the doubts of our courage to fight

The white supremacists throughout our continent

Our neglected acts of rebellion will now be in your face
Exposed for all of our people to embrace
The forgotten women
Belittled and overlooked since 1492
Seen as mere commodities for the invaders to enjoy

Stealing our land, infected us with smallpox
Purposely, killed 95% of our population
and here we are claiming a Spanish grandfather
Ashamed of who we are, bleaching our hair blonde
popping blue eye contacts
Concha Nacar selling us skin bleaching creams
to burry away our identity
we are the forgotten women, this is our war cry
Hear our war cry, we the forgotten women
This is not the story of Pocahontas
Not the story of Malinche, not the story of Chel,
from Road to El Dorado from Steven Spielberg,
This is the true story
Women warriors of this occupied nation
In 1492, We rather commit suicide then have our vaginas
stabbed with venomous dicks
When we met the original motherfuckers in 1492, in 1519
They forced fucked our mothers and now we are supposed to believe that it was a love
story, sprinkle some hearts, and a pink back drop and the rape scene is supposed to
look like a honey moon retreat
bullshit

We are the women that resisted

We were doctors, poets, teachers, merchants, writers, priestesses, mothers, daughters,
grandmothers,

In Tenochtitlan, in Cahokia, in Caral, in Bolivia, in Guatemala, Hopi, Dineh, Tongva,
Chumash

Daughters of corn, masters of time, calculating each time a child was born
We planted the original seeds of civilization, our corn
Now faced with the destruction of our peoples nation

We are those women that are ignored by the Europeans writing because they were
disgusted to see us educated, handling our shit, meanwhile they burnt their women at
stake for the study of medicine
1492, 1519 came to us like a lightning

To burn through our cities and our humanity

We women, the original women of this continent
Did not just stand there, did not just sit there

Actions hidden from your view because they don't want to give you any ideas of what it means to resist
Indigenous Nican Tlaca women warriors all over our continent
we are the forgotten women, this is our war cry

We are those Mexica women that during the bloodiest battles against the Spaniards, dressed up like Mexica warriors and fought the Europeans and they massacred us
We are those Indigenous women, who rather commit suicide then be raped by them
We are those warrior women whose arms they chopped
Whose babies they stabbed in our bellies as we fought
We are the forgotten women, this is our war cry

We are the Incan Warrior, Lorenza Avenamay, whom the Spaniards called "la india del diablo" who was decapitated for organizing uprisings against the Spanish crown: 1725

we are the forgotten women, this is our war cry

We are the Inca warrior, Manuela Bastidas, organized rebellions, and for her courage she ended up with her tongue cut and strangled, public execution : May 18, 1781

we are the forgotten women, this is our war cry

We are the Tongva warrior, Toypurina, helped lead a rebellion in Mission San Gabriel Arcángel

Who said upon been put to trial

"I hate the padres and all of you, for living here on my native soil, for trespassing upon the land of my forefathers and despoiling our tribal domains."

**We are Toypurina, standing in the cold room,
October 25, 1785**
 we are the forgotten women, this is our war cry

**We are those and many other warrior women, who remain nameless, because they want their colonization to continue painless and blood-free in their version of white history
White supremacist is shameless**

But their poisonous lies won't tame us

The normalization of our genocide is beyond sadistic

Let me remind you, let me scream at the tops of my lungs

See these Obsidian blades shoot out my mouth
we are the forgotten women, this is our war cry
Slice through this matrix of white supremacy
That has us on our knees
And willing victims in our own genocide, you know what I am talking about, brown on brown genocide
See these Obsidian blades shoot out my mouth
Mexican, Central American, Native American, South American
My beautiful people of this continent
They want us to sleep deep in their Trans
They give us the American dream
As we wake and face the nightmares of their colonial reality
Our pride left empty, our hearts left bruised
We are buried in deep in the veins of this colonial monster
We are homeless in our homeland
Went from the most educated people in the world
To the highest high school dropout rates
Use their colonial terms like Hispanic and latino, to blend in into their identity scheme venom and accept the lie that tells us we are illegal on our own lands
Hear our war cry, we the forgotten women,

Let us live in you today, tomorrow in your future,

Hear our warrior cry! Let these blades of obsidian tare through the lies that keep us sedated and hypnotized
Hear our warrior cry!
Toypurina, Manuela Bastidas, Lorenza Avenamay, Frida Kahlo, Maria, un-named warriors, un-named heroes,
HEAR OUR CRY!
They didn't finish with us all
They couldn't possibly kill us all
We are the survivors of the world's biggest genocide
Making a comeback to what is ours,
520 years will pass on to be a memory of the period in time when we were blind, lost, and confined to colonizer created ignorance!
See these Obsidian blades shoot out my mouth
Show you the rage of a people locked in a cage
Built with their bones and fed their own blood

Hear our war cry, we the forgotten women,
See these Obsidian blades shoot out my mouth
See these Obsidian blades shoot out my mouth
Our aim is to defend our occupied continent
Hear our war cry
Hear our war cry
It's time to put an end to this GENOCIDE!

2013

Watch my video version of this poem:

http://www.youtube.com/watch?v=rlwJLTtVOZw

What does White Supremacy make us think of ourselves?

Overly sexualized, dumb, dirty, self-hating

DURING INVASION: HIDDEN HEROES

We have been resisting their terrorism since 1492

"Women were frequent participants in and even, on occasion, leader of colonial rebellions. William B. Taylor has written,
Militiamen called in by the Spanish authorities were likely to encounter nasty mobs of hundreds of women brandishing spears and kitchen knives or cradling rocks in their skirts, and young children and old people carrying or throwing whatever they could manage, we well as better armed groups of adult men...In atleast one-fourth of the cases, women led the attacks and were visibly aggressive, insulting, and rebellious in their behavior towards outside authorities."
(p.141 Indian Women In Early Mexico, Schroeder and Wood)

Black and Brown Unity March Los Angeles, 6/2007

YOUR LIES, 4th of

Stole our land
Killed our people
Enslaved us and our African brothers and sisters
And claimed your White independence on this newly stolen land
Keeping us in shackles
Writing your bloody documents that solidified and justified to your motherland that now
you were on your own
Leaching off our people
Living off our people
But according to you independent
What a lie
What a myth
Constructed for your own morality
You continue to be captive
Of your own illusions
Nican Tlaca resistance
To your white supremacist traditions
Today we gather to discuss your ongoing occupation
And our upcoming liberation

2011

What Compromise

I am not going to compromise who I am for the fraudulent perverted expectations of what a woman shall be. I am out to fulfill my dreams for a better future of our people, ain't no man, no job, no bullshit going to dictate to me what is worthy and what is important. I ain't your traditional, catholic brainwashed, self-hating, insecure woman. It's a new day and women of Cemanahuac are warriors at a whole new level.

2013

KKKORPORATE LIFE

this corporate world is fucking robbing me of the energy to continue
their deadlines
their greed
 their hypocrisy
the more you work the more they take
 math all day my worst subject
 a racist ass White emotionally
unstable over-seer yells
 cries
all fucken day
this kkkorporate matrix is breaking my head
 I surround myself with our warriors in my walls
I keep my eyes on the prize but there are
Days
where I see the reality of my office as a cage
unwritten poems sophicate my heart
I write words in my mind
and at the end I try to find time to vomit this spell
 and then my mind wonders into a future where I can be a teacher but to get there
 I must shatter this world before me
since 18 I am on my own no funding from the fam most didn't give a damn so I was
forced to become an adult
reject becoming a foster youth and fully embrace my truth
today I am more sick then I was yesterday
 today I see the veins of this reality ripping
before my eyes
the kkkorporate world is a tool to captivate our time fuck this system
 I wanna rhyme my time with thing truth that swims in my mind
I am fucken tired of being the hardworking independent slave woman
shatter this chain shatter this pain

2013

27

YEAR 521

521
years of resistance
witnessing the destruction of our nations
521
521
fighting
being killed
persecuted
raped
occupied
521
521
each year the pain is sharper and the needles of lies dig deeper into the archives of the shame of European savagery
521
we will make you remember year 1
we will make you taste some of that anguish
stand before you and never walk away
1492 is our 911

Día de La Raza? Que nos pasa

Con este lenguaje salvaje que me han forcado hablar
Tal como el ingles pero hoy en este me voy a enfocar
Quiero vomitar esta ideologia que me esta cayendo rete mal
Dejenme decirles que estas mentiras yo ya no puedo soportar
Hace 521 años vinieron a dañarnos
Los invasores del mundo europeo
Un hombre perdido llamado Cristobal Colon
Declaro estas tierras propiedades de sus reyes con permiso de la iglesia catolica
Mirenlo que bonito nos rèsult este pinche cabron!
Y miren hoy como celebramos el disque descubrimiento de nuestras tierras
Celebrando el robo de nuestras riquezas
La violacion de nosotras las mujeres
Una nueva raza?
Una nueva mezcla?
Una Raza cosmic?
Sin saber que ese concepto de Raza Cosmica fue creado para celebrar lo europeo
Manipular lo indigena
Dicen por ahi

Que deberemos agradecer a los europeos por su conquista
Que eramos rete feos
Pinche racism que existe en nuestras casas
Sin saber que fueron ellos que nos mataron en millones
70-100 millones de nuestra gente
Holocaust
Genocidio
Racist y immoral
Mestizos? Que va!
Una violacion no merece una celebracion
Nuestra historia no empezo con la invasion
12 de octubre, día de la raza,
Raza? Ni que fueramos animals
Pues claro como no teníamos nada de grandeza
Ni una civilisacion de mas de 6,000 años
Pero al instante que nos invadieron
Quiero que nos pongamos al brinco
Nos infectaron a proposito
Con enfermedades letales y ahora pretenden
Que todo fue un accidente
OOPS! Ay perdon!
Que triste que sea muy comun ser racistas
Cuando nacen nuestros hijos
La suegra se queja
Que esta muy Morena!
Pregunta que si tieno ojos de color
Que no la tengan mucho tiempo bajo el sol porque despues se va aver bien indita
Que desgracia!
Que verguenza!
Ni cumplen un año y ya empieza el daño
El racismo de este colonialism
Y la tele
Ni se diga!
Las oxijenadas son las dueñas y las morenas las sirvientas
12 de octubre
Día de la Raza?
Que nos pasa!

Donde esta nuestro coraje?
donde esta nuestra inteligencia?
500 años de colonialism no nos quita nuestra herencia
Pero canal 34 dice que España es la madre patria
Cristina y Don Francisco que somos latinos
La Opinion y telemundo que somos hispanos

Tenemos que ponerle un alto a estas mentiras
Tenemos miles de años en este continente
Hemos visto a casi todos los presidents
Decendientes de los originales invasores
Desde Mexico, Centro America, y sur America,
Casi puros criollos gobernando!

12 de octubre es un día de Resistencia y coraje
No de pachanga y danzantes
Día de la raza?
Que nos pasa!

2010

Watch my video version of this poem:

http://www.youtube.com/watch?v=r4fBGsxlJmU

PROTEST COLUMBUS?

Because we love our ancestors
 because we love our people
 Because we love truth and justice
Because 521 years is far too long
 Because 100 million of us were killed but they live in us
 We are them
We descend from them
They are us
Each one of us is their memory
We must honor them
 we must honor the unknown warriors
 the thousands of uprisings
 we must honor them
 in honoring them, we honor ourselves
 We live a little more with their courage
We are alive but days like these make our life more meaningful
 make our life a weapon and today with our life,
we make sure the world remember them

2013

More info:

http://www.youtube.com/watch?v=hDPVpTzbFec

32

AT AN EARLY AGE

at an early age
found myself locked in my rage
asking why i had to see and live what i did
stuck in between the morality of lies
at an early age
i learned about death
i asked why and found the answer in questions that went unanswered
dared to speak out against the shit that happened
ran away every chance i got
rebelled in the justice that i knew was mine
at an early age
my eye lids were ripped open
forced to see the venom
that crawls in blood streams
at an early age
i grew old
had to crawl out of the cave of hopelessness
to find who i was
letting others thoughts limit my potential
i was a a danger to the illusion
i spoke truth and didn't care to be casted out
at an early age
i learned i could choose my destiny
stay down and bleed
or rise and heal

KERNELS

I woke up in a bed made of corn kernels and turqouise
I woke up with a 4000 hummingbirds dancing around me
I woke up in a garden filled with instantly blooming roses
I woke up in a pool filled with floating acatrazes
I woke up with Nahuatl numbers being sang to me
I woke up with chocolate earrings
I woke up to the sound of my thoughts breaking through mental glass

Do you remember me?

Hi
I don't think u remember me
Yes we've met before
I mean
I at least should seem a bit familiar
You see
I used to be yours
I was your eyes
Yours ears
Your mouth
I dressed you
Nurtured you
I used to be your pride and your
Strength
I know where you came
I knew where you went
You loved me
Embraced me

I thought we'd be together forever----------------------eternally
I matched you in every imaginable way
Your brown skin
I was the decibels that bounced off your tongue
You used to say my name with love, respect, and admiration
Exhilaration even
Determination
You proudly displayed me on your clothing
Jewelry
You read me
Studied me
UNDERSTOOD me
Celebrated me
Scientifically
You knew me
I was you and you were me
BUT NOW.........................
But now it's like if you don't even want to acknowledge me
You ignore me
Degrade me
Hide me in bleach
You avoid the beach
And when you see my name on the check off list
You brush me off and pretend that I do not exist
You act as if we have no history
Like if I never defined you
Your existence
Your providence
U ignore any evidence that would glimpse at our
United relevance
Now.
Now you rather go by that other name
Praise that other color
because it is whiter
Oh!
I mean BRIGHTER
No offense
You swear you and I never me
That your features have nothing to do with me
You deny that we ever shared a history
You want to keep my presence a mystery
BUT AS HARD AS YOU TRY TO HIDE FROM ME
I RUSH DOWN YOUR VEINS
I SIT THERE IN THE BACK OF YOUR BRAIN

I AM YOUR LAUGHTHER, YOUR PAIN
THE DRUM IN YOUR HEART
YOU CAN'T DETACH ME

I AM IN EVERY KERNEL OF THE COB THAT YOU EAT
IN EVERY JUICY TOMATO THAT IS BLENDED INTO YOUR V8 DRINK
IN EVERY BEAN THAT IS SMASHED
IN EVERY INCH OF THE LAND BENEATH YOUR FEET
IN EVERY "0" THAT IS WRITTEN
IN EVERY DECIMAL POINT OF A FRACTION
IN EVERY STAR GAZED UPON
MY SWEETNESS MANUFACTURED INTO THE WRAPPED CHOCOLATE IN YOUR POCKET

I MAKE UP EVERY CELL IN YOUR BODY
I AM IN EVERY STRAND OF HAIR
IN EVERY PORE OF YOUR BODY
IN EVERY BREATH THAT YOU TAKE

I AM IN YOUR MIRROR
I AM THE ROOT OF YOUR FAMILY TREE
THE UNFAMILIAR WORDS THAT YOU SPEAK:
AHUITES, TOCAYO, CHICLE, CHIPOTE, ZACATE, PAPALOTE, EZCUINCLE
COYOTE, ELOTE
ALIVE
But buried in the depthness of your mind
I am always present, have always been here
But dug deep underground
Profound bound to your chains
Living unrecognized
Rejected neglected
INFECTED WITH YOUR HATE

I AM :
MEXICAN, CENTRAL AMERICAN, NATIVE AMERICAN OR
OTOMI, PUREPECHA, HUICHOL
I AM:
PIPIL-NICARAO, MAYA, MEXICA, CHUMASH, NAVAJO, HOPI
I AM:
SALVADOREAN, FROM HONDURAS, NICARAGUA, COSTA RICA
NICAN TLACA, INDIGENA
BLEEDING IN YOUR MEMORY
KIDNAPPED IDENTITY
AND THEN BRANDED INSULTED WITH

HISpanIC, LATINO
YOU SPIT ON ME
SLICE ME
PISS ON ME
SHIT ON ME
WHEN YOU MISTAKE MY IDENTITY WITH FOREIGN CONCEPT S AND ETHNICITY
I'VE NEVER ABANDONED YOU
I SURROUND YOU
BUT U TRY TO DROWN ME
NOW,
DO YOU REMEMBER ME?
I'VE BEEN RIPPED OFF FROM YOUR BRAINS
WHEN YOU WERE PUT IN CHAINS
WHEN RAPED
SLICED
WHEN OUR BABIES WERE TORN IN TWO BY DOGS
HAS IT BEEN THAT LONG?
FOR THOUSANDS OF YEARS
YOU AND I WERE ONE
BUT NOW
AN OCEAN OF BLOOD DROWNS YOU IN LIES
I'VE BEEN KEPT FROM YOU
AND U
U HAVEN'T EVEN BEEN GIVEN A CLUE?
THAT YOUR LONELINESS
CONFUSION,
IGNORANCE
IS KILLING YOU
KILLING ME
I AM THE ANCIENT
YOUR PAST
YOUR FUTURE
WE ARE INSEPARABLE BUT TEMPORARILU BREAKABLE
FOR MORE THAN 500 AND STILL BREAKING
HOLD ME
RECOGNIZE ME
LOVE ME
YOU ARE DYING
YOU ARE DYING WITHOUT ME

2004

Jennifer Juarez from the Mexica Movement

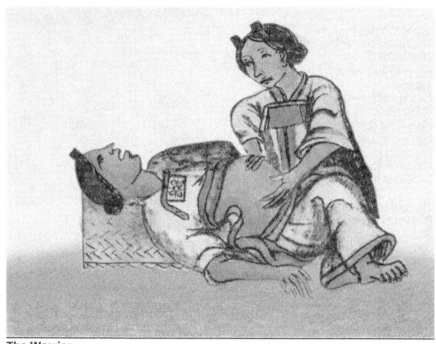

The Warrior

In that womb he laid
Weeks and months
He laid
Arms and legs developing
Brown skin wrapping itself around his body
Like a gift
Waiting
Waiting to embrace the world
In that warm belly he laid
Weeks and months
Waiting for the embrace of the world
As he was waiting and waiting

They were sailing and sailing
Planning and sailing

He waited and waited

But they were coming, running
Sailing through the oceans
They were already on their way
They landed
Roaming and burning
Stealing
Raping
Lying
Destroying our cities
Running through our temples

And as he waited
As he waited

The cold tip of the sword sliced away at his shelter
Piercing his body
Sliced his body in half
Chopped
Chopped again

His flesh dangling
Half in the womb
Half out into the world
His mother laid dead
She could not run
In a puddle of blood
Chopped off her feet
Chopped off her arms

She could not embrace him

They lied and said that they came in peace
Meant no harm
BULLSHIT
Lies lies lies

This is not what he awaited for

For his mother did not squat and birth him
For his mother was not celebrated for giving birth to a future warrior
For a priestess did not welcome him
For a priestess did not explain to him what role he would play in our society
His umbilical cord was not wrapped on a small shield
He was not bathed in the fresh water of Chalchitlicue

He was soaked in the blood of his own body
Soaked in the blood of his mother
Soaked

His body dropped
On the bloody ground of Tenochtitlan
Body dropped on the ground of the beautiful city
The beautiful city that was
No longer

His blood ran and soaked the shield of this father
Skin ripped off by the fangs of the dogs
His life taken by the hands of monsters
He was waiting in the womb of his mother

To be hugged
To be born
To learn the science of corn
But those monsters did not care
They ran crazy with their swords

Intentionally spreading diseases throughout our cities
Knowing we had no immunity

European invaders year after year
Century after century
More blood poured
More lives stolen
More lies told
More children devoured by dogs

In our heart the warrior waits
In our heart he is alive
She is growing in your heart
She is growing in your mind

Developing courage and strength
Alive in each one of us
100 million are alive in us

Pump our blood
We are that warrior
We are not dead

We have arms
We have legs
We have courage
Knowledge
Strength

We are not dead
We are that future warrior
That mother
That father we are Tenochtitlan
We are Cemanahuac

The blood stops here
The lies stop here
Raise your mind and hearts
In this space and in this time

We are that warrior
We are that warrior

2010

Watch my video version of this poem:
http://www.youtube.com/watch?v=9sMaqhc9ZtI

Inevitable reality

no matter how high the build the border
how many laws they try to pass
our people are here to stay
learning the truth of the settlers and squatters

the fear is near
they start to shit tears
using bullshit rhetoric to pretend they care about "America"
when in reality it's the INDIGENOUS people on the comeback

you see, after 500 years of genocide
there are over 1 billion of us missing
due to the invasion of our lands
yet they don't seem to understand
our population growth
is inevitably more

our land has been sliced
poked and stabbed
and we are treated like illegals on our land of birth
borders on our land are cuts
superficial boundaries that are temporary restraints
on the reality that is crawling through history

here we come
here we go
back to what is ours
don't you know
my people are waking up
and giving a fuck
looks like the colonizer is out of luck

occupation can't be stuck in our history
the era of colonialism will soon only be a memory

we are full blood and mixed blood INDIGENOUS people
NICAN TLACA
from Mexico, central america, north america, south america
nican tlaca

its inevitable
its predictable

but we have to keep learning
we have to reclaim who we are
we have to break the chains
stop being so blind to the pain
disguised in alcoholism
teenage pregnancies

its inevitable
its inevitable

2011

Nican Tlaca Future

Poem To Be Read After Our liberation

Let's fast forward to a time where we are free
let's fast forward to a classroom where our children are no longer put back to sleep
lets fast forward to the Anahuac Nation, our people free from Occupation!

****

i want this poem to be read when we are no longer the living dead
i want this poem to be read when we are free from self-hate
when we no longer allow ourselves to be called HISPANIC, LATINO, RAZA, and
MESTIZO
When we gain back our independence and still look out for all others

I want this poem to be read when our little girls no longer question their beauty
when they look in the mirror and love what they see
when the media represents who we are without any fallacy
I want this poem to be read generations to come
when we have the right to walk all over our lands freely
when the constitution reflects our cultural rights
our citizenship rights Anahuac citizens

when we speak our languages
Nahuatl becomes the national one
I want this poem to be read, when it needs to be translated
because we no longer speak as slaves of Europeans
I want this poem to be read in a classroom
surrounded by proud beautiful Nican Tlaca youth
I want this poem to be read
as we build alliances with all the free nations
I want this poem to be read as my sisters and brothers no longer oppress each other
with machismo or feminismo
when that isn't needed
when we create our own future
i want this poem to be read when we are not limited of our potential
cultural centers are built in every city
we know who we are just like every proud ethnicity

I want this poem to be read by my great great great grandchildren
who will remember their grandma and they will be proud of me
that i thought about them
before i even had my first child

49

I want this poem to be read
when we rise from the dead
and break from the graves
of the cells in our heads

i want this poem to be read
when the whole world acknowledges the genocide that take place
five centuries hidden from the memory of our collective history

I want this poem to be read
long after i am dead
because i know that i will live on
in the hearts of our people
and in this time that I was placed in

i want this poem to be read
when we no longer are lead by white supremacy
in our jobs, in our homes, and in our institutions

i want this poem to be read
i want this poem to be felt
i want this poem to be sang
i want this poem to be whispered
i want his poem to be a memory
of our current condition

2014

An Ocean Within

I opened up my heart today to discover that i have an ocean of love stuffed away in my
arteries
from the love that i receive
from the support that i receive
from my mentors who have seen me grow

the limits are only in my mind
only in my imagination
though i am not where i would love to be
i am a work in progress
and i strive to become more than what i was yesterday
better than i am today
stronger than a year ago

the ocean woke me up today
the waves of inspiration
i am making my own victory

i do not fit a social standard
i will learn in my own time
i will complete school as i have time
i will grow with everyday

so long as i am honest
i will make honest mistakes
so long as i am sincere
i will never put myself on stake
so long as i speak from my heart
i cannot be a fake

this is where i am
this is what my progress has been

Everyone has impacted me
Every conversation
good or bad
every memory
good or bad

and in this ocean
i find myself swimming
i need to learn how to swim
not allow myself to be hypnotized by the matrix

i have an ocean within
limitation is only my imagination
i thought i was free
but now i realize that it is just the beginning

i love this
i want this
i want to live this
i want to nurture this

Anti-THANKSGIVING DAY

Fasting for thanksgiving to denounce the lies of such a day
to denounce the glamorization of our genocide
the cover up of white supremacy
the denial of our humanity

as the turkeys are being stuffed
the potatoes are being smashed
my people getting drunk in "gratitude"
no food will enter my body

not today
this i do to remind myself
that i have been given the life of knowledge
that i see with the eyes of truth and the eyes of my heart

protesting with my body
with my heart and with my mind

Many cultures/religions fast as a way to show sacrifice
to remember
to discipline
to show love to the Creator

as a colonized people we are not there yet
we do not have defined ways of resistance
that shared collectively as a people
but we can try

we seek liberation in our daily lives
we speak education in our daily lives
we seek decolonization
and after more than 500 years we still have a long way
but every day that you live try to get closer to that reality
with every book that you read, action that you take
decision that you make may it be in the benefit of our people's future
may it be in the benefit of our liberation

none of us are perfect
being born into this white supremacist matrix
robs us of being disease free
but we can try to cleanse ourselves daily
with living with a refreshed sense of resistance
and discipline in our education
in our liberation
in how we treat one another
sisters
brothers

it's a beautiful thing to know the truth of who you are
it's even more beautiful to know that our liberated future gets closer
the more we reach out to our heritage with the courage of
 Cuahutemoc and the
 clarity of Zapata.

may your day be filled with
courage
and truth

2011

Unlocking The Mysteries of Histories

I ain't the brand name on my clothes
nor am I your clone of criticism
this is who I am
in my time
and in my prime
I don't need bullshit standards of beauty to repress who i was born to be!
I ain't what i own
I am who I know
with each day i grow
plant your seed in my soul
let's go explore truth and make history glow
with the light that we shed on five centuries of mysteries
picking up the books that didn't make it through
the pages of textbook filters
redefining what it means to be alive and make it
searching for the truth and not having to fake it till i make it
too many needles poking at my brain
trying to penetrate the thoughts that keep me sane
if this is the only moment we get
we will fucken work our asses off to make sure
they regret, erasing our glory from our hearts
and stamping us with the ink of lies
we are ripping off the forced disguise
of a people who just live
consume and die
I see the strength in us everyday

strong enough to be the slave
yet ignorant till we end up in graves
that shit is changing
I see the matrix breaking
piece by piece
by tools of courage
invisible weapons of mass education
the true enemy of our people's damnation
their resistance to our takeover
their bullshit borders
becomes a cotton wall
and with it we make our clothes
come one come all
this gear is for all
the big the small
the short the tall
we ain't brand names
nick names
colonial games
this shit ends with us
now
they can't figure out how
we can do this without guns
how we can accomplish our dreams
without going back to sleep
they are paranoid
afraid
cannot understand our rage
constructing plans of liberation
that require the violent thoughts of uprising
with educated minds
and hearts
this is a whole new way to make waves of change
redirect the ocean of lies that drowns our pain
I am proud to know the truth
at least the little that has awakened my mind
to fly into the realm of imagination
and know that our years of freedom
are just a few generations away
let's keep our minds refreshed
awake
and
alive

2012

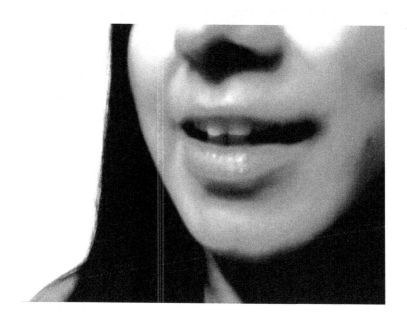

WORMS IN THE HEART

Ever so often i have to perform open heart surgery to remove the worms from my heart.
little white creatures that suck the blood from my four arteries and seek to devour my soul by occupying my heart
Last night i stood up till 3am
I had to do surgery
I am recovering from their invasion.
Hoping i got rid of all of them.
I cannot allow my heart to decay in the mental mazes that are created by others' expectations of what it means to be a warrior and an Nican Tlaca woman on the rise.

I feel refreshed and renewed
I feel prepared to lift my weapons from the bloody battlefield of inaction and the dreaming worlds that suck our blood like mosquitoes in the dark

I thank you for letting me find myself again and again
 No one is immune to die

A reflection on my pilgrimage to Chichen Itza

Sticks and stones can break my bones
but mathematically aligned stones that create monuments to the Creator will make me
stronger
Chichen Itza
i visited your city today
As i walked through the colorful entrance,
as i made my way by the vendors, in my mind
i saw you light up
i saw your red colored platforms
flowers surrounded your doors
As i walked to this city
i remembered my ignorance
how i saw your relevance as a distant relative
and now through the years
a connection now stands
where an empty mind was
a strong warrior now is
where a confused heart existed
a warrior one now beats
in awe of this city
of what we created
of how well connected we were to the Creator
we could only try to build our city in rhythm with the universe
with the glimpse of galaxies
trace the veins of our existence in stone
i did not burn sage
i did not do a dance

i cried
i remembered
i appreciated every moment
and i looked around
our people present
mainly vendors
meanwhile tons of Europeans, Aisans,
admiring
and those of us who remain ignorant to our glory
confused at their admiration
and those of us scarred
 thinking we have no connection
and those of us that gave up
thinking there is no future for our culture
and then there was those of us Nican Tlaca
who stood there
in amazement
we said THIS IS OUR HERITAGE
i can see the pride in our peoples faces
bursting with smiles
cameras rolling
flashes
i wanted to capture this moment
i wanted to freeze time
and just let my mind imagine
allow myself the chance to recreate this city
in its prime
in its time
in its sacred place
in its scared moment
in its planning
and its building
and the engineering meetings
in the labor
i wanted to allow my mind to dive into its history
grab all of the inspiration
and just bury it in my heart
so that i can carry it with me for decades.
i stood there,
although i have much more to read
although i have much more changing to do
i stood there
and accepted myself
my flaws

my strengths
my goals
my failures
my victories
i accepted my present
i embraced my past
and i was exhilarated for what is yet to come
i stood there
thankful
craving more discipline
craving more knowledge
but thankful for everyone who has planted a seed in my mind
for every experience that has allowed me to cherish my time on this planet
i stood there grateful
overwhelmed by the mere shadows
the education that lays embedded in each stone
each calculation
and there our buildings stand
and there they stand
naked
tall
alive
how many millions of our people
never got to witness our glory
how many of our people die without ever knowing who they were
how many of us live our lives in shame and in constant escape of our culture
of our heritage
i feel refreshed
i feel thankful
alive
and stronger
being there alone will not change the world
but being there for me pushed me to change my people's future
to push myself
to revamp myself
to grow more
to speed up my healing
to dive into courage
to allow myself the imagination of a new dimension
to tare down the walls in my own mental cages
and spread my warrior wings over the new challenges before me
Tlazocamati

2011

The Katt house slave

I used to laugh at your jokes
watch your DVDs
recite
"THIS SHIT RIGHT HERE"
cus that shit was funny
that shit was hilarious
talked about you to my friends that had never heard of you
and then bam
Boom
you spat in my face
SHIT
Diarrhea
you went insane
We should've fought for California?
 while we were being killed in the millions?
raped
Purposely infected with smallpox
we "lost" it?
you lost your sense of dignity
A BLACK man bent over for white lies
This SHIT RIGHT HERE
was Stolen!
1492
1519
1848
STOLEN!
Go back to Mexico?
really?
can't really go to a place that exists where we stay
can't really go back and fix what the Europeans have destroyed and continue to
operate!
we have been here for thousands of years
more than 7 minutes
you vented
danced around in a Circle
like a puppet
invisible strings parading you
U.S.A! U.S.A!
You act like America didn't steal you from the motherland
kill your ancestors
drowned them

tortured them
in the millions
Malcolm X, i bet, is turning in his grave!
KAtt, you got lost in the white man's paper
in the white man's drugs
thankful to the master
you now joined his dance
Meanwhile he don't give a fuck about you
about us
but your cash
your self-hate
your brown hate
keep fueling the black vs brown
Don't you know how many of our people die killing eachother
Black on Brown crime
Brown on Black crime
and you don't give a fuck!
you enjoy to see us fight
blaming each other for the realities we face
over 500 years of genocide
and rape
it pains me
how the crowd cheered you on
and you came to that sound
you busted a Kramer
and we are supposed to take that shit?
we are supposed to just accept it and laugh
I am glad you let us know where you stand
waving the blood stained American flag
next to your puppeteer, the White man
ooh! how proud you make white supremacy
conquer and divide
an old trick with new guinea pigs
A house slave cheering on the master
This shit right here
This shit right here
is RACISM
WHITE SUPREMACY
you don't have to be white
to be a white supremacist
I wonder what Dave Chappelle would say?
You a rich bitch with chains

I made a youtube video responding to his racism:
http://www.youtube.com/watch?v=QRQMjBIAyA4

http://www.youtube.com/watch?v=_NynvCXcFxA

BEST
Do the best with what you have to help further our people's liberation. I am not perfect and have a long way to go in my growth, but I won't let any of that stop me from speaking out. This is the information that woke me up, this is the knowledge that gave me essence, and i want to share it with the world. Mexica Movement is a culture of resistance, university education, philosophy, self-help, true mental nutrition.

Loving to Live
there was a time that i thought love only came from a particular person
at a particular time
and before i knew it i was left blind
by my own neglect of the daily rays of love that come my way
it's taken years to see the love that crashes into my path
but i see now
to live i must love
and the more i see love the stronger my life becomes
to struggle for our peoples liberation
there is a love of our culture, a love for our people
a love that is generations in the making
sprinting towards space and time
but nevertheless it is coming
to love who we are
where we are
and to love what we know
to love why we know it
and to love our purpose to show it
live it
love it
now i nourish my mind and soul with the love that awakens my existence
warriors are tough
but we love with the same passion that we fight

NO SOMOS MALINCHE!

No Somos Malinche
No Somos Malinche
No Somos Malinche

Somos mujeres guerilleras
defendiendo nuestras fronteras
desde que invadieron los monstros
del Europa y de las tierras de las gueras

Somos guerrilleras volando con alas de Cuahutemoc
viviendo con valentia de Cuitlahuac
sabemos defender nuestro bello Anahuac

No saben nuestros nombres
porque los hombres blancos
nos mataron antes de preguntarnos
Nos mataron nuestros hijos
antes de darles luz
nos mocharon las manos
antes de agarrar nuestras armas
nos han dejado el corazon en llamas
almas robados buscan justicia negada
y volvemos para gritar
y volvemos para ensenar
y volvemos para vivir
para pelear
somos mujeres de Anahuac

No Somos Malinche
No Somos Malinche
No Somos Malinche

no saben de nosotras porque
nos borraron
no saben de nosotras porque
eramos de guerra
luchando diariamente
para la liberacion
de nuestro continente
nuestro continente

usaron nuestros cuerpos

invadiendo nuestros vientres
y exijian mas esclavos
que gente tan demente
pero nosotros no
nos dejamos
nosotras
peleamos

no dejemos que nos separen hoy
no acepto que me dicten quien soy
a donde voy
bajo que lucha moriremos
somos mujeres de Anahuac
al extremo

Pocahontas
era usada
explotada
usada como payasa
en las tieras de los invasores
violando mujeres menores
sin rencores
sin verguenzas
no les importaba nuestra dignidad
sociedad
nacion
vida
muerte
puro chingar y chingar
puro matar
violar
infectar
infectar

podriendose su propia humanidad
y nosotras viviendo
defendiendo
armando
peleando
recordanod nuestra lucha
y ahora solo se acuerdan de malinche
como si nuestras vidas no importaran
como si nuestras vidas no valoraban
somos mujeres guerilleras

dando nuestra vida
para terminar las pesadillas
de esta ocupacion
fatal
somos mujeres
en guerra

Watch my video version of this poem:

http://www.youtube.com/watch?v=2sfrPOhn_Hg

MULTIPLE HEARTS

I have multiple hearts
my heart was under a microscope
sliced open it dripped blood
cut in four slices
and still it kept beating
and still i kept breathing

the black mud was poured out
and it still had its beat
it still bled

they kept slicing
and like cotton candy
it was just fluffy
red

and beating

they dissected it
dug into my arteries
and it still bled

i was not dead
i just laid there
with my eyes open
and the cold air just blew through my hair
i was alone in the night
staring up at the moon
as they keep dissecting my heart
i could not fight
the coldness of their thoughts
just kept tearing and slicing
my flesh

looking for robots
looking for secret maps
and they did not find anything
but blood
and pieces of turquoise
pieces of memories that remained stuck
permanent

like a tattoo on my heart
they could not tear that apart
and frustrated they ran away
frustrated cus it wasn't there

sliced in four pieces
bleeding
the mud poured out

glistening in the presence of stars

they did not get far,
i have more hearts stored away in my mind
and i recreate them every time one dies

so they dissect and dissect
and only inspect the physical one in my chest
meanwhile my real hearts float in my soul
like fish in a tank
like oil on water
like leafs at the park

Veronica Thomas and I protesting Anaheim's racist and corrupt police. 2012

If I rise and fail

If I rise and fail
I will rise again
If i fail to rise
I will never win
i have let go of all
just to view within
into another view
vision of a union
with my ancestors dreams
when i fall to sleep
i rise to wake
among the reconstructed cities of our lands
and i run through forests filled with new directions of liberation
smiles and cheers
welcome new year's
new time
new space
to regenerate what was lost
and rebuild our strengths
buried away we collect the millions of umbilical cords of unborn warriors
and attach them to the future
buried away
we dig up shields
that were shattered in the the battlefields
buried away
we dig up the courage
that was stuffed down our hearts and sealed away in silence
if i fail to rise
i will never win
the battle of our liberation
is just about to begin
rise to the future
grasping our past
embracing the unity
from past
from present
from future
we will rise again
cus if we fail to rise
we will never win
but if we rise and fail
we will continue

till the end
cus there is no failure
just lessons tied to our experience
warriors wake
courage wake
it's not just the land we're taking back
it's a whole new world of thought
it's a whole new world of action
rise to win
win freely what is ours

2010

A REALITY

Not a struggle but a reality
there comes a point where the struggle for liberation becomes part of your being
your mind is always thinking of the long term effects of your actions
you read the truth
you go to work
you pay your rent
and before sleeping you read chapters of American Holocaust

You don't call yourself Hispanic, Latina, Raza, mestiza
you represent who you are
you don't have a virgin de Guadalupe frame in your room
and you don't apologize for not speaking perfect Spanish

you understand liberation will take all of our collective action
you love
you live
you dance
you smile
you hit the gym
you eat some bomb ass mole
you come home
do some yoga
you don't go to church on Sunday
you seek peace in truth
you thank THE CREATOR for allowing you to breathe
than for allowing you to think
than for allowing you to fight
the struggle becomes an honor
loses its traumatic sense
it's a daily fight
that you love
because you know it's the way to live
to have substance in your path

2009

Reclamando

Pase lo que pase
Le Cueste a quien le cueste
Estamos reclamando a nuestro bello continente

Caminando en nuestras tierras diariamente
Creando la consciencia que libera nuestras mentes
Estamos conscientes
que cada pulgada de este continente
nos pertenece
nos pertenece
Cada verdad que aprendemos nos fortalece
Con cada protesta y marcha, nuestra valentia crece
Pase lo que pase
Le Cueste a quien le cueste
Estamos reclamando a nuestro bello continente
Somos Indigenas, nuestra identidad es Nican Tlaca
No somos gavachos, anglo-sajones, ni americanos
Nuestros heroes no son Washington ni Lincoln
No somos democratas ni republicanos
Somos una nacion bajo la ocupacion
Somos los duenos de lo que tanto desean reclamar
Pero digan lo que digan
Lloren lo que lloren
Esta tierra no se la van a quedar
El nombre de America se la cambiara
Anahuac, nacion de los originales regresara
Esta justicia sera con educacion y accion
Nos la llevaremos con calma
Sera una revolucion llena de armas mentales
No se trata de convertirnos en lo que fueron
Y usar armas fatales
Las balas no matan la verdad
La violencia mas efectuosa el la que nunca se usara
Nuestra presencia
Demuestra la esencia
De el merito de la Resistencia
Despues de 500 anos
Hemos sobrevivido
El plan de genocidio
Hemos demostrado

Que nuestra lucha no se quedo en el olvido

Pase lo que pase
Le Cueste a quien le cueste
Estamos reclamando a nuestro bello continente

Seguimos estudiando nuestra herencia entera
Mientras ellos se esconden detras de su pinche bandera
Sangrando con nuestro sangre
Manchando su himno nacional
Esta realidad no se puede evitar
Diariamente nos gritan que somos ilegales
Cuando la verdad que les quema es que somos originales
Los ilegales criminales son europeos invasores
Ocupando nuestras tierras por mas 500 anos
saqueteando nuestros recursos y violando a las menores
esto no es America, es nuestro bello Anahuac
somos las hijas u hijos de Citlalmina, y Cuitlahuac

Pase lo que pase
Le Cueste a quien le cueste
Estamos reclamando a nuestro continente

Estamos exponiendo la verdad escondida
Regresando la verdad a nuestras vidas
Mexicanos y centro americanos
Somos hermanos
Somos hermanas
Dividieron nuestras tierras y esclavisaron nuestras pueblos
Quieren que renunciemos a nuestra identidad
Y que ni levantemos un dedo
Pero ya se esta oliendo su pedo
Las mentiras pudren el alma
Como desean que odiemos nuestros origenes y regalemos nuestra libertad
Pero estamos regresando a lo que nos pertenece
Estamos reclamando lo que el europeo no merece
Reclamando nuestra humanidad
Rechazando la brutalidad colonialista
Somos una nueva generacion que esta lista
Marchando al ritmo de liberacion
Viviendo una lucha con dedicacion

Pase lo que pase
Le Cueste a quien le cueste

Estamos reclamando a nuestro bello continente

Deunciando los terminos colonizadores
hispano, latino, raza, y mestizo
esos terminos los hechamos al pizo
es el Nuevo plan que han establecido
es un hechizo que no tieno oficio
Somos Nican Tlaca, indigenas de todos los colores
Sangre pura, sangre mezclada
De nuestra identidad, solamente nosotros somos los autores
Guerrilleros y guerrilleras con armas en la mente
Educando a nuestra gente diariamente
Creadores de civilizaciones originales
El maize dio luz a nuestro paiz
Pero en ignorancia ignoramos la verdad que esta ahi
Fuimos la gente mas educada del mundo
Ahora nos quieren atarantan con Univision y telemundo
Pero te lo aesguro
Pase lo que pase
Le Cueste a quien le cueste
Estamos reclamando a nuestro bello continente
Estamos alzando las caras y las almas
Para demostrarle al mundo que seguiremos resistiendo
La calma se muere cuando la pasiencia te mata
Escucha el Corazon latiendo en tu pecho
Es la presencia de Emiliano Zapata
Pase lo que pase
Le Cueste a quien le cueste
Estamos reclamando a nuestro bello continente
Pase lo que pase

Le Cueste a quien le cueste
Estamos reclamando a nuestro bello continente

2011

SB 1070

so let me get this clear
i walk around
i am brown
i live in Arizona
i will get asked around
they will frown
they will clown
and i must carry my papers with me
everywhere i go
to the park
to the store
i will be checked like a child
in the hallways
like a lost puppy
if i walk around in AZ towns
i will be a suspect of being "illegal"
they can all stop me
tare down my self-esteem
ask if i have the white man's permission to exist on these streets
cus i am brown
i will be locked down

if i don't put down
the papers on their hands
should i tattoo my social security card to my wrist
to my forehead
should i make a patch
wear it everywhere i go
to be seen
like a watch
to be spotted and inspected from afar
so they don't make a fuss
and ask around
if i am brown
in Arizona
i am gonna be a slave checked by the mastahs who own her
everything Hitler did was legal
legalized racism seems to be the sequel
Arizona can't take the fact
that we are a people on the comeback
our homeland is borderless
yet they continue to be memory-less
of where they stand
of what land they are visiting
of what future they are fearing
because i am brown
i am asked to categorize my humanity into terms that their legal systems understand
stripped of my rights
my voice
and my mind
i can foresee the future
forced to wear chips in our bodies
rounded up in legal camps
designated areas where we can walk freely
they can come into our homes without probable cause
and just check if we are legit
as our children's sleep
this is deep
if i am brown in Arizona
i am a target of racial profiling

My beautiful grandmother Mercedes and I

Ser Mexicana

SER MEXICANA ES SER GUERRERA
MIRAR EN CADA COLOR UNA IMAGEN DE NUESTRA CULTURA
SER MEXICANA ES ACORDARSE DE LA BELLEZA QUE REFLEJA EL NUEVO AMANECER
SER MEXICANA ES AMARTE A TI MISMA
POR TUS RASGOS INDIGENAS
PIEL MORENA
PELO NEGRO
OJOS COLOR DE CHOCOLATE
DE NO AVERGONZARTE DE TU HERENCIA
SER MEXICANA ES UNIRTE A LA LUCHA K TODAVIA NO SE ACABA
DESPUES DE MAS DE 500 ANOS Y SEGUIMOS COLONIZADOS
SER MEXICANA ES RECONOCER QUE NOS HAN ROBADO NUESTRO CONTINENTE Y
SER MAS QUE CONCIENTE SINO SER UNA PARTICIPANTE PARA LA LIBERACION DE
TODA NUESTRA GENTE
SER MEXICANA ES SIEMPRE TENIENDO EN TU CORAZON Y MENTE A TU BELLA GENTE
NUESTRA GENTE K A SOBREVIVIDO EL GENOCIDIO
LA MASACRE DE NUESTRA CULTURA
PERO ENTRE LA SANGRE ROBADA SE ENCUENTRAN LOS GUERREROS K NUNCA
MORIRAN
SER MEXICANA ES MAS QUE UN ORGULLO ES UNA RESPONSABILIDAD COLECTIVA
SE K NO PERTENESCO A MI SINO A MI GENTE
SOLO SOY UN INSTRUMENTO
UNA ARMA VIVIENTE PARA LA DESTRUCCION DE NUESTRA OPRESION

2007

I really care but....

you see
i like what you are doing
its really cool
protesting and learning the truth
seems like really cool things to do

you see i really care but
i have to go to school
i have to work
i don't know how to get around
i am sick today
i really can't go

you see i really like what you are doing
but i have to record my album
entitled REVOLUTION
so i really can't make it to the protest
but i will thank you in the CREDITS

you see i really like what you are doing
but i am on my own
i am more of a solo person
can't really follow anyone
cus i already got all the answers
i just ask cus i am curious

i really like what you are doing
and i would donate
but i gotta get my rims
and than go gamble on the weekend

but i give you props
keep it up

i would go but it's too hot
i would check it out but i need to get a pedi pedi
i mean
i don't think i will be done in time so go ahead without me

i really like what you are doing
but i don't have time

i really support you
but i can't be involved

i really like what you are doing but it seems too serious
i like to have fun
and not stand with a sign hours long under the sun

i really like what you are doing
maybe i can use your materials
and make shirts and stickers and sell them
cus i want to spread the message
but i really can't go to the protest

i really like what you are doing
maybe i can take pictures of your event
and use them in my portfolio
cus i am looking for a job

i really like what you are doing
maybe i can tell you where to protest
and what to chant
cus i really can't go out there myself
its too weird
not as cool as me

2014

Rodeada

me la pase rodeada de guerreras y guerreros
todos animados con el alma en el continente entero
horas llenas de verdad y direccion
risas seguidas por conceptos profundos y buena conversacion

sin mamadas o sangronadas
estamos enfocando nuestro futuro liberado en soluciones
basadas en nuestra condicion de colonizacion

rodeada de armas
corazones con balas
amando el futuro que ce acerca con nuestras fuerzas
hicimos historia
aunque el mundo ignore nuestra presencia
la historia de resistencia se hace con dedicacion y persistencia

pura alegria
entre la seriedad del dia
porque tratamos con los temas que tanto nos han negado

historias robadas
tiempo olvidado
sangre invisible
corre del pasado

cada uno de nosotros
somos los que escaparon
la muerte segura
planeada y que se ejecuta

rodeada de guerreras/guerreros
mi alma se alimentaba
anos de liberacion
renacieron en mi corazon

mi heroe hable de accion
que rezar con merito es la solucion

me econtraba en un dia
que nunca llegaba

con gente que parecia suenos

humildad
valentia
honor
conocimiento

estamos en preparacion
para reclamar lo que es nuestro

corazones llenos de armas
armas de honor
armas de guerra
armas de defensa

somos la nueva generacion
que se rebela

acciones son nuestras balas
nuestras palabras son dedicadas
a el futuro que se acerca

a nuestro liberacion
que viene poco a poco

asombrandose en la historia que esta por ser documentada en la memoria de la
existencia

Thanking him now: A Poem Dedicated to Olin Tezcatlipoca

Timexihcah
You unplugged me from the matrix,
for that I will always be grateful.

as a a teenager you gave me some knowledge that made my heart cry and my mind expand.
For that I will always be grateful.

You helped me realize my strengths and my weaknesses
Gave me harsh punishments
But because of all of that i am here now

We don't have the institutions to give you your place.
You have made a warrior society in our minds.

Over 30 years of being a active in the defense of our people we will always be grateful.

And just as you have seen me grow and become an adult
I have also seen you grow and become a Tlamatini.
An educated and fierce Elder.

I saw you walk with your cane, and it breaks my heart
to accept that you are aging
yet so many more ideas in your mind and fire still burning in your heart
I must assist you in that growth
that continuation
in that spark

life has made you a living hero

humble
fierce
awake

nobody knows true sacrifice like you
nobody knows true commitment like you

I thank you now.
again and again

for waking me up
to a life of dignity and courage

I have no shame and crediting you
in giving you your proper credit
what i write and how i fight
how i speak
is all a reflection of your training

Ometeotl,
Ometeotl
Ometeotl

Tlazocamati Olin Tezcatlipoca

Nitlatoa niyollotl

8/23/10

86

Know the Truth!

**1492:
White Men
Raped
Indigenous Women**

**Sexual terrorism, biological warfare, and violence by
Europeans have created
Amerikkka.**

www.mexica-movement.org

It's over!

It's over
this bullshit acceptance of our demise
the forceful glued eye sockets melts with truth
it's over
with every action of resistance what we take
we bring forth the new generation of women who are going to take it all back
picking up the shields that lay scattered throughout Anahuac
building up our force like a puzzle
you are a piece of history made into flesh

we are the new warriors breaking away from Eurocentric myths of womanhood
we are not Malinche

we are women warriors
learning our history
Devouring the pages of lies that are tattooed on the lining of our minds

Let's leave behind the farce of joining the politicians
our children are growing faster than we can repeat this
and after five centuries we will not dare live like this another decade

taking up actions of liberation
mental weapons shooting truth to shatter blindness
bruised knees from where we used to be
our existence will be measured by our courage
 this is a new type of warrior society

we will not stay home as we are in war
we will not worry about what is going on in the battlefield
we are the battlefield
we are the war
we are the weapons

women of Cemanahuac
this is ours
our time on this planet
on this chunk of our land
we need to save it
understand it
be fierce and awake

my heart shakes when a lie breaks like glass
shattered underneath my feet
as i walk through this darkness
the truth is the light within our minds
nourished through time
books
life
and lessons
wrapped into one

Women of Cemanahuac
i dedicate my life to our voice
to our fight
If we were in Tenochtitlan in 1521
we would be the ones killed for planning the attack
we would be the ones burnt alive

for resisting their venomous dicks
we would be the ones
non existent

but here we are now
here we are now
working
going to school
learning the truth
protesting
laughing
living
loving
 fighting
we are fighting
with our daily lives

It's the new uprise that takes
every moment of our lives the be realized

no longer are we hypnotized
by anorexic bleached shit
thought to be ugly
inferior
a sex tool

fuck that!
we are the new warrior society
we are the women of Anahuac
with no apology

I express this with the pain
of being brought up in ignorance
seeing my peers be the witness
of brown on brown genocide
teenage pregnancies

making decisions
about our survival
ego's out of control
Opportunists always had the floor

but this shit is over with
this new age phenomenon is pointless

we are the flesh of this resistance
we are the flesh of this battle

we are the womb of this birth
birth of liberation

2011

5 Centuries
Five centuries of occupation will only be a scab on our existence as a people once we all
collectively recover from the damage of this colonial world that rips out our humanity
and rapes the potential out of our minds and hearts

2010

LATE NIGHT

I am up late night
feeling good
thinking
Remembering
what i have lived through to be here
what i have learned
to be here
what i have thought

cried
laughed
and i am thankful
for all of it
yes i am thankful to see it
build me
nurture me
for i was not given the love of a mother
nor was i given the presence of a father
nor was i given the love and care of a family
but i have been given the love to see it
to find my family in people who connect my veins
to see the strength in my pain
to see my life before me
and doing my best not to live in vain
i see it
i am thankful
i am not living the life in the Hollywood family structure
but i am managing
i love my friends
my warrior nations
my mentor
my childhood
my best friend
my heartbreak
my love
my journey
the puzzle that i try to build
every night
the canvas that is being painted on
Everyone adds a color to this mural
every drop counts
and with this
i have learned to find peace
to search for truth
cus i am not alone
i have been guided
i have been nurtured by many mothers
i have been guided by many fathers
and i have loved
and cried
fallen
fallen
risen

risen
and i am thankful
for this moment
i am thankful for this time
i am proud of what i have
i am proud of the love that pours from my heart
because it gets nurtured by many oceans
oceans of people who live for the future
who smile
who protest
who read
write
fight
and don't lose sight
i love
thank you

Small groups of people make history

Small groups of people make history
small groups of people can tear shit up
We don't need millions
We don't need thousands
Just a small group of people who are committed and dedicated
No one said it would be easy
We must sacrifice the toys
sacrifice the emotional drugs
the matrix hugs
We must stay away and AWAKE from the spells
not fall into the traps of politicos
or the stupid saying that goes like this...
"Ain't nothing gonna change anyways..."
stupid apologist excuses for non-action
small groups of people
small groups of people can cause a revolution
a liberation
a complete re-direction

of where our lives will be in the next generations
African slave trade was resisted and destroyed
by violent uprisings
small groups of people rising
Women's rights movement, began with a handful of women
who decided to take control of their lives and create a voice
small groups of people
small groups of people
dedicated
committed
willing to do what it takes
some may complain
WHY DON'T PEOPLE TAKE ACTION UPON LEARNING THE TRUTH?
Well history tells us that it has been a small group of people who organized new worlds
and i ain't talking about elites or oligarchies
i am talking about a small group of people
WILLING TO DO WHAT IT TAKES
WILLING TO GO THROUGH TJE UPS AND THE DOWNS
THE EMOTIONAL STRESS
THE POSSIBLE DISAGREEMENTS
BUT COLLECTIVELY DECIDING OUR NEXT STEPS
Look at Bolivia, Venezuela
Small groups of people organizing
Educating
Sacrificing time
chunks of their lives
for a better collective future
a prepared collective
for a liberated future
Free Future
Small groups of people
Small groups of people
Who remember what it meant to be BLIND
to be lost
the be guided by the poison of colonialism
and who woke up
Small groups of people
who will see themselves in the eyes
of all of our people
who still sleep
snore
Hypnotized by the lies
Tirelessly driven to study
to teach

to challenge
to change
to confront starting with ourselves
IN THE MIRROR
small groups of people
can liberate
can revolutionize our lives
dedicated
committed
focused
alive
it only takes a small groups pf people
to get the ball rolling
and once the ball is rolling
it will start smashing lies and deceit
small groups of people
small groups of peple who have purpose
and
KNOW THE VALUE OF TIME
THE VALUE OF SPACE
WHAT IT MEANS TO BE ALIVE
AT THIS VERY MOMENT
TAKING ADVANTAGE OF THE TOOLS BEFORE US
TO CREATE AN OCEAN OF RESISTANCE
TO CREATE AN OCEAN OF IDEAS
EXECUTING THE PLAN FOR LIBERATION
No one said it would be easy
No one said it would not hurt
but the outcome is far beyond beautiful
it's medicine for all of our souls
small groups of people
small groups of people

small groups of people

like us

2012

Watch my video version of this poem:
http://www.youtube.com/watch?v=h4MIzp9TZDg

Never again

never again will i fall to my end only to discover i became my own best friend
doubted and twisted
they thought they had witnessed the demise of my mind and the destruction of my soul
and i burst through their frozen shit thoughts
i promised our ancestors i would never get locked up by my own limitations
the indoctrinations of fear and self-hate
everyday i escape the claws of statistics and the dreadful end of resistance
i owe all to my mentors, my teachers, and my enemies
this fire i breathe is kept up by this need to shake up the matrix cell
trying to use this life to give them hell
sometimes i whisper
at times i yell
it all depends on the situation and how hard it is to tell
what will shift
what will happen next
the stabs in my back are now only reminders of why i don't turn away from the enemies
i stay in place
and keep this rhythm
Everyday i hear new melodies
crawling into my heart and rock me to sleep
if i ain't alive then why do i breathe?
bleed?
it all comes with this battle
ain't gonna paint it all pretty
never again
will i witness another fall
and stay motionless
shocked and in pain
i am no stranger to tears
i often rain
only to cleanse my soul
to refresh my eyes
to not lose my mind
to not lose my heart
attached to me
i try to be
a stronger warrior
another type of person
i won't get tainted
by the insecurities of my environment
i want this moment to last an eternity
but everyday i am getting close to the end of me

so meanwhile i am here
let's smile
and fight
Let's resist this system that drips with our blood
and tries too hard to make us give up.

never again.

SE PUDRE

hay algo en mi que se pudre si no hablo
hay algo en mique se muere cuando trato
 de negarme la verdad
de mi pasado
lagrimas estoy cansadade evitarlo
 ay algo en my que se pudre si no hablo
es mi direccion que aumente con mi depresion
 no encuentro paz en la religion
 en la supersticion que nos a encadenado
no encuentro paz en la danza de payasos
faltando respeto a lo sagrado
 hay algo en mi que nace cuando muero
una de me gente en ignorancia y mugre
mentiras respirando lodo en nuestras mentes
hasta el punto de llamarnos insurgentes

hay algo en mi que se pudre si no hablo
la frescura de la verdad
tenemos que demostralo
 hay algo en mi que fallece cuando duermo
ideas de mundos y gente en infiernos
pidiendo perdon al Creador por pecados
anitguos como colonizacion
la gente muere dormiendo en su rencor

hay algo en mi que se pudre cuando callo
la verdad de mi gente tengo que expresarlo

2012

Watch my video version of this poem:
http://www.youtube.com/watch?v=W_vO3g7zrKs

99

CHOICES

so many choices to make
so many voices to fake
Illusions of another day
what is at stake
if i take the other way?
how much less work would i have to do?
how much less hours would i sleep?
 if i think things through
it pains to see decisions ending
 in blood
on our own hands
stains of guilt stretched out spread out in prisons
teenage memories
of death streets
body parts scattered like flowers at the funeral
like stars imploded
nothing beautiful lasts forever
nothing beautiful lasts forever
living life as a dream when a war that does not end
a life without a soul
no beginning
just end ending it ends everyday
choices
voices
 choices
voices
what will help us
what will damage
what is suicide
what is selfish
what is righteous what is honor
what is dignity
who do we look for for guidance in this matrix hell
where neighbors fiend for drugs
kids cry at night
junkie parents
selfish college educated young adults
trying to get the fuck out of the hood
cus brown people ain't no good
cus there ain't never enough food
choices

choices
voices
screaming
whispering
secrets of answers that i cant decipher
just upset at this situation
what more to give up sanity is vanity
revolution is not enough
choices
dark thougths creeping
when you see all of this it just hurts too much
it paint to see our own weakness manifested
undressed
naked in the mirror of justice
in the mirror of humanity
what will judge us if not our actions
what will blind us if not our own illusions of visions
self help spirituality masturbates emotion
and does not guide action
i am sick this ache in my heart
this ache in my mind
this ache in my spine
this ache in our time
this ache in our time
how much more do we have left
choices
voices
your own sound
your own mind
reacting
teasing
pleasing messing up the future
my fingers fall off one by one as i count the times i thought i knew how to use my tools
my weapons
a soldiers worst tool is his own gun

VEINS

as the darkness of pain creeps into the left of my brain
i am left to decide what choice to make
so i'll slice through the veins
of the matrix with rage
until i find myself sucking life from a new heart of strength
hot tears melt scars down the cheeks of the vain
and depression dances in the outline of beautiful thoughts
branded insane
same brand given to great men and women of truth
who since their youth of teared down walls of lies and deception
and although bloody and bruised
still get up from the chains of the worst type of slavery
the slavery of cowardice
for there is no perfect warrior
just the attempts
and that is all that matters
as we grow older
until we lay permanent in the memory of humanity
we must use our existence with a violent passion to change what is coming
by changing ourselves
as i slice through the veins of my own cage
i remember the words of my guidance
to always do the right thing
even if it hurts in silence
cus the world will never know
how much blood had to pour
to renew a soul
from the slow death of inaction
from the slow death of a new direction
discretion
with our lives
for they are borrowed from the universe
and any one of us can be plucked out and thrown into the ocean of
millions of souls that froze in selfish dreams
frozen souls in ice that never melts or makes it to the riverbanks
just frozen
Stagnant and broken
no matter how hot the sun
or cold the nights
the fire must continue to heat the warrior within you
to continue to do the right thing
so fight free

fighting
starts
within
healing souls
no one knows
if ever cured
only words
hear you
change
at death
we know
how much we really did
until then
fight
fight
fight
fight

Ain't here to be

ain't here to be your celebrity
look anorexic like those playboy bitches you masturbate to
ain't here to be your pedestal Mexican queen
who will wear the latest fashion
always smile and be ready to serve you
ain't here to be victimized by your insecurities
ain't here to just listen to your talking shit
Meanwhile you expect me to sit back and pretend its constructive criticism
ain't here to profit from my work
my philosophy nor my passion
ain't here to spit gossip about so and so's sex life
or who got botox
ain't here to be what i am not
ain't here to be your emotional disposal can
ain't here to be your academic robot
ain't here to be your stereotype of what it means to be a warrior
ain't here to retract the harshest facts of being colonized
ain't here to please no one but our ancestors
ain't here to be perfect just a Nican Tlaca woman on the rise
ain't here to be a puppet for your own projects
ain't here to be sucked of my love for my people
myself
and my family gardens
ain't here to be molded into your perception
ain't here to be told i cause disruption
ain't here to eat your shit
ain't here to dance in your piss
ain't here to serve you
ain't here to deserve you
ain't here to be what i am not
not a mexica diva
not a wanna be self-made fashionista
this is the time where i was given to live
this was the space i was given to breathe
this is the fight i was given to free
ain't here to get rich
ain't here to be your brown bitch
ain't here to be a mannequin
silent
cold

Replaceable
ain't here to fear
ain't here to tear
ain't here to smear
here to love
here to fight
here to bring meaning to my life

JESUS CHRIST DID
NOT DIE
FOR ME.
MY ANCESTORS
DIED
FOR ME.
www.mexica-movement.org

CAVES

We will not crawl into your cave of hate and watch you bury our humanity away into the pits of your guilty conscience. We are the walking dead resurrecting from five centuries of resistance. Genocide is not enough to delete us. We are coming in the millions, making up for the billions of us that are gone due to your greed and demonic ideologies. Fear is not an ingredient in our liberation recipe.

My great grandfather was Huichol not a fucken Spaniard

www.mexica-movement.org

*Stop claiming a white ancestor. Take pride in your Indigenous bloodline.

BORN

this system we are born in
is supposed to keep our steps dictated
our thoughts sedated
our minds filled with selfishness
our actions are supposed to only benefit our pockets
we are born into web made up of our veins
we are given plastic balls stuffed in our sockets
we are supposed to live and die in their ideals
we are supposed to bleed their greed
 we are supposed to want to marry them
have light babies
fuck ourselves to death
but this system can only exist in our own limits
this system is only alive because we are the walking dead
we break our backs
we serve their desires
we die for them to live
but this system is fading into the corpse in our minds
we get life
we begin to live
when we realize that we have been dead
the pulse of our people's liberation
pumps clear
i feel it
the air is fresher
the water clearer
our blood redder
our eyes open
and like a baby gasping her first breath
our hearts gain a new strength
we are supposed to be a statistic
a failure
we are supposed to kill each other for street credit
get high everyday
fly away in our minds from our truth
we are supposed to buy the big house
drive the new car
Participate in the system
that recycles our sweat

that uses our blood as gasoline
our land as its toilet
but truth is the option
is the key
is the medicine
statues become flesh
we are supposed to
stay down
ashamed
ignorant
what a beautiful day it is to change
It's never too late to participate in your people's future
what a beautiful day it is to know the truth
what a beautiful day it is to tell our young how beautiful they are
what a beautiful day it is to breathe in our existence
to resist
to love
to laugh
to read
to protest
to live
to dive in our purpose
we are supposed to exist
and thats it
we are supposed to live hollow lives
and that's it
how beautiful it feels to know what reality is
how beautiful it feels to unleash your potential
on the future of our peoples liberation

we are supposed to be just another name in the grave
just another social security number
just another consumer
how beautiful it feels to breathe freely
think freely
act in liberation
to know

What is

poisonous tears run down my cheek
as i sit here and think
of all the fucked up thoughts i used to have
about my self
my hair
my skin

poisonous tears
that run down deep
remembering the self-hate that
was buried in my heart
my mind asleep

Poisonous tears run deep
burning holes in my cheek
remembering when i wanted green eyes
and light hair
just like my 10 lil barbies

poisonous tears
cus i didnt know any better
even the characters on Sesame Street
had blue eyes
and through those eyes
i wanted to see this world
that hated me

poisonous tears
i wipe
with thoughts of love
i bathed in our ancient civilizations
and am cradled to sleep
by the Nahuatl lullaby that i know exists
i know was sung to our babies

poisonous tears i wipe from my young sisters eyes
hug her tight
and show her the glory that is hidden from her view
history books can only hide so much
a new horizon awakes her
a new mentality now shakes her
a new found courage now makes her see

beauty in knowledge
Beauty in truth

Poisonous tears
i want to disappear
no more pain accompanying our history
break free from this venom

beautiful little Nican Tlaca child

2010

Reservations

The cities that we live in are all reservations,
the worst parts of our lands
next to toxic dumps
our buildings built on toxic foundations!
 Environmental colonialism
 health hazards
every block
stained water
brown air
another way to keep our people dying
white supremacy keeps on breathing our life everywhere
if we don't die from gang violence
we die from cancer
stuffed into apartments
poverty is a colonial manifestation
white education
self-hate
no self-worth
we are headed in the wrong direction
mark my words
there isn't a coincidence
there is no true connection
that we just so happen to be the ones dying
the ones crying
the ones begging for survival

tired of attending funerals
of people who could've lived longer
could've been stronger
if we had justice in our lives
from our minds
to our bodies
tired of reading how many homicides
brown on brown
homies representing streets they don't own
a pride that no matter how much they swear they have
leaves them pointless and empty
reserving a spot on our lands
for our slow destruction
our slow death
generation after generation
passing the chains of self-hate
along the umbilical cord
our children born into the shit
that awaits them to hate
themselves
reserving our lives
to suck our resources dry
 and state that we are still here
that they respect our rights
just to feed into their modern ways of genocide

history pages filled with new faces

year after year
we are waking up
thankful for the opportunity to rise up
meeting new people that are glimming in knowledge
thirsty for more truth and blossoming in courage
year after year
i see smiling faces
shake hands with new warriors
and share beautiful experiences
each one of us burning a whole through the matrix
leaving our mark in the unwritten pages
history stands by our side
the air of justice gliding through the words that we speak
concrete facts breaking hollow lies

112

empty arguments
quickly shattered with evidence
we speak clearly
we walk with pride
every year I meet another me
I meet another you
and together we march down the long alley of hidden truth
exposing lies
evolving into a full collective
every year I am renewed with inspiration
waking
fighting
walking
learning
Thank you for waking up
thank you for keeping me awake

2006

<u>Eternal</u>

I feel eternal today, I feel in love with our future, I feel alive today! I feel that we are making way for a new life to begin, I feel honored today, I feel grateful, I feel connected to a part of me that is yet to be created. I feel LOVE today, I feel pride, I am swimming in my heart and imagining the unthinkable!

2005

114

Where Is The White Humanity

I broke free from the stone skin you caved me in
to be a memory on humanity
a scar of your conscience that shatters and bleeds
a scar that never heals
a history that you hate to reveal

I stand in your face
look you eye to eye
you look down as you try to trace
where you left the last chunk of your humanity

did you leave it in the sword that you sliced me with?

115

did you leave it in the corpse that you burnt alive?
did you leave it in the vagina of my mother as you raped her
did you leave it in my father's limbs laying lifeless on the streets
did you leave it in my broken temples
did you leave it in the oozing puss filled lumps on my peoples skins dying in the stench
of smallpox

or did you lose it on the shore?
did you lose it as you sailed back and forth
and each time you returned
less human
less you
To make less of me

Where exactly did you leave it?
How exactly did you get it?

An ocean of blood
I will force you to drink

Force you to eat the dirt where you buried our hearts

Where did you leave the last chunk of your humanity?

did you leave it in the constitution?
in the Atlantic ocean?
in the 23 million faces

look at me
i am the millions that no longer are here
missing from this earth

missing
like your humanity

2013

Watch my video version of this poem:

http://www.youtube.com/watch?v=D42LpPzs4g0

Listen Sisters

Sisters
Sisters
We've been told that our own men
Are an oppressive mold
Who take hold of our lives and dreams
And yes that is true for many cases
And yes that is true for many instances
But we cannot hate them
For being men
Being FAKE WHITE MEN
Acting like WHITE MEN
Acting like WHITE MEN TREAT THEIR WHITE WOMEN
Dividing ourselves up even more
Our oppression as women is intertwined with out brothers
We are all victims of colonialism
colonialism
is flesh and blood
poverty
death
divisions amongst a people
By fake borders

Fake obligations
Fake subjugations of our names
Our identities
We the women of Mexican, Central American, and Native American descent
We are full and mixed blood Indigenous women
We are full-blooded and mix blooded Indigenous women
We are ancient women trapped in White solutions
We are ancient
As Ancient as the Olmec
As Ancient as the Maya
As Ancient as the Zapotec
Teotihuacan
Ancient
ANCIENT WOMEN TRAPPED IN SELF HATE
ANCIENT WOMEN TRAPPED by WHITE DREAMS AND DESIRES
MEANWHILE OUR EXISTENCE IS DRENCHING WITH EXPERIENCE
FIERCENESS
COLLECTIVE LEADERSHIPS THAT HELD UP CIVILZIATIONS
Ancient women who walk on their own land
And don't know it
Ancient women who created beautiful philosophies and don't show it
Ancient women who are beautiful in their brownness
Light brown
Dark brown
And don't know it

We planted seeds
developed corn
We studied medicine
We were doctors
Priestess
We were educated
We were liberated!
We were one!
We were free!
When they were in Europe!
We were free!
We were teachers!
When they were in Europe!
We were writers!
When they were in Europe!
We were poets!
When they were in Europe!
We understood the creator!

But in Europe
they burnt their women for studying medicine
Forbade education if you had a uterus and went through gestation

Now
we are separated!
We have been raped by the white man
Racially sexually
Terrorized
assaulted
And our men are fine imitators of the genocide perpetrators
And now we are told to glorify Malinche
The woman who voluntarily assisted the enemy
Fucked him in treason
And fucked his men
We don't know of our TRUE warriors!
The women who fought Europeans
Who rather commit suicide then to be degraded by rape
To be stabbed by venomous dicks
Being stabbed for over five centuries
They had no right to our bodies
They had no right to our lands!
They had no right to make us slaves!
To chop off our hands!
We fought Europeans
We warrior women and men
Fought Europeans
As a people!
Women picked up shields of f the arms of our dead warriors and defended our lands
We defended our people
This is the hidden history of the women descend from
This is the real women we should honor and imitate!
Writers
Priestess
We are seen as uncivilized
Exotic, dolls of white pleasure,
Sex tours gone wild
as
White chicks crawl out of mansions and beamers
Inherit stolen lands
Stolen wealth and invite us to be equal
That will never be
Until their men are equal with our men
They tell us we suffer the same and that we should have the same solutions

That they understand what it means to be oppressed cus they are women
Same women who owned slaves
Same wife to witness genocide
their hands are just as bloody
Just as bruised
Just as dirty
COLONIALISM CAN ALSO BE FEMALE
MATERNAL COLONIALISM HAS GONE UNNOTICED
Sisters!
Fight for our
Stolen nation
It's the white man
It's the white woman
We must make a call to war
A call for warriors
Men and women warriors
soldiers
And take a look at our men now
Not all but some
It hurts to see them
Drunk
It hurts to see them beat on women
Depressed
Just robots for labor
Robots of the Europeans
Victims of false standards of power and a twisted view of manhood
Self-destructed in alcoholism, domestic violence, social imposed inequality
Based on the behavior of white men
How do we explain
That before they came
We were both educated
Sharing professions in medicine
Theology
Legislation
The sciences
Art
We can be that once again!
WE WILL BE THAT ONCE AGAIN!
Unite!
Correct yourselves brothers!
Unite!
Correct yourselves sisters!
Let's fight it out together!
Unite!

I'll be damned if my people don't get free
I'll be damned if we let another century
Slip us by
And yet we are still in slavery
My enemy is not my brother
My enemy is not my sister

Watch my video version of this poem:
http://www.youtube.com/watch?v=S3rFM2AJpCc

2008

My beautiful sisters Angelica and Yesenia 2012

121

Olmec Heads Speak

Today Olmec heads become alive and scream
Discussing what is to become our reality
enough bullshit already with this colonial scheme
we've been here observing the whole deal since 2500 bCe
seen them put you all to sleep 500 years,
i wish i can get up and help you see, the truth our heritage starts with me
the other Olmec head responds with a smile:

but look, they are awaking, and defending our pride
our ancient existence is now displayed up high

WHEN LIBERATION IS HERE:

flipping thru channels I just heard them announce
LAUSD kids did not attend class for October 12
denouncing it as a genocidal holiday
Columbus represents death and no parent wants their kids to participate in that myth
Disney is banned for crimes against humanity and promoting and distributing white
supremacist products
Power Rangers become Zulu and Mexica Warriors
Simpsons begin episodes on how to start a Bolivarian Revolution
The Statue of liberty is replaced by Frida Kahlo, standing tall and beautiful lifting a
codex in her right hand and a Mexica Shield, just like her earrings on the left

children refuse to pledge allegiance, as early as elementary
And when asked
We won't respect that which disrespects us
making us beg to be treated equal when it is our land on which they continue to steal
and perform their occupation sequel
cus this is reality hitting home
we are waking up
500 years of sleeping in ignorance
dying in ignorance
comes to an end
our hearts begin to beat
to the rhythm of our liberation
we begin to live again

we are waking up with courage and knowledge
streets names get changed to reflect heroes that resist

123

Gage becomes Cuitlahuac
Cesar Chavez Blvd becomes Emiliano Zapata
Florence becomes Doreteo Arango
Atlantic Blvd becomes Anahuac
ELAC
Gets a statue of Cuahutemoc to replace the husky
we paint murals that educate our people with none of that gangster shit
our kids listen to Dora, la exploradora,
new episodes she explores ancient Nican Tlaca, Anahuac culture,
and she sings in Nahuatl
sings in nahuatl
Her name becomes Xihuitl
and she continues to dance and sing
BATE BATE CHOCOLATE
BATE BATE CHOCHOLATE
MI GENTE INVENTO EL CHOCOLATE
SOMOS MAIZ
SOMOS FRIGOl
SOMOS LA BELLA GENTE DEL SOL
SOMOS MAIZ
SOMOS FRIGOl
SOMOS LA BELLA GENTE DEL SOL
BATE BATE CHOCOLATE
meanwhile Diego becomes Cuachic and he sings in Nahuatl
and he counts in Nahuatl
CE OME YE
NAUI MACUILLI
CHIQUACE CHICOME CHICUEI

Clairol blond hair dyes, go out of business
cus my sisters discovered true beauty
And bring their self-love back to existence
and start to witness
a love for their culture, their image, and their past
black hair brown skin
embracing our melanin
no longer live confused by diverse shades of brown in our community
we understand that scars of rape of our people
and WE DO NOT IMITATE WHITENESS
We are FULL AND MIXED BLOOD INDIGENOUS PEOPLE!
We understand that Mestizaje is an hechizaje to keep us from loving ourselves completely
blinding us to worship white gods and white supremacy
magazines now had a new look

124

the new generation of brown beautiful proud youth
with stencils of mayan art filling up their sporty jackets
revised huaraches with glittered Mayan glyphs
We are an educated people once again
turquoise becomes our gold
education system mandates by
POPULAR DEMAND to teach ANCIENT ANAHUAC
And our stolen lands
beginning in Kindergarten
playgrounds become replicas of Chichen Itza
our children slide down the temple of Quetzalcoatl
and swings carved like MAYAN art
la placita olvera becomes our Museum of Resistance
Showing the true side of missions and the genocide committed
depicting the heroic acts of our people as we gained independence
Museum of Tolerance creates a new section for our genocide
Exposing the genocide 70-100 million of our people that were killed
we are slowly making up for the lives that were stolen
Census Bureau reports that the majority of the United States of what was formally
known as America are of Mexican, Central American, and Native American descent
The NICAN TLACA option is created to reflect our population
building cross-cultural alliances with the African (or better yet KEMETAN) community
creating defense groups that report white supremacist terrorism to the new United Free
Nations,
All of Tenochtitlan is excavated and renovated, buildings take on new architectural
wonders
after Palenque and Bonampak
replicas of the temple of Quetzalcoatl and Toltec warriors are removed from the Forest
Lawn cemetery and placed in the new historical PLAZA ANAHUAC, formally known as
Atlantic Square
every mission becomes a cemetery, museums of genocide
we are actually a community
you can sense the unity
helping each other out
no longer the crabs in the barrel
establishing cultural centers
honoring our existence
computer labs
homework centers
arts and crafts
making sure that we have what it needs to fulfill our potential
TO FULFILL OUR POTENTIAL
TO FULFILL OUR HUMANITY
no more BROWN on BROWN

BLACK on BLACK
BROWN on BLACK
BLACK on BROWN
we are united and tearing down
white supremacy
can you see LOU DOBBS frown?
can you see the statue of Pete Wilson being tore down?
and there are even new modern-day John Browns
who fight white supremacy among their own kind
what? put that shit on rewind
Malcolm X speeches are memorized and analyzed for 8th graders
we no longer worship in the religion of the Raiders
we correct the terms used to identify us
NO LONGER do we ALLOW TO BE INSULTED with
HISPANIC and LATINO,
Raza and Mestizo
you get a ticket for using colonialist jargon
today!
make it a reality!
today!
i do not talk of an unrealistic dream
today!
this is real if you know the truth
the inevitable celebration and creation of our nation
a peek at what's to come
of what is now
of what we can do
of what
will
be
done

2008

On Extremism

Extremists? radicals? The only extremists are those that go around killing people in the millions to obtain material and false psychological gains. Stealing lands, slavery, and cultural rape are extreme actions of White Supremacists. Those of us who fight back are merely defending our existence and our right to a liberated future. Go call someone else extremists because you definitely don't understand the most violent occupation in the history of this known world.

2012

Life and Death

life is a daily gift that constantly unwraps itself before us. don't be afraid to peel inside and pull out the magic that is hidden from your eyes. Dig deep inside and bring out the turquoise flowers that are growing in your heart. None of us are perfect, but each one of us has the magic to evolve.

2011

Resistance

August 13,1521 has been documented as the Fall of Tenochtitlan! Let's remember that date but as the rise of more warriors! Those that went down fighting, nameless to the Spaniards but not to our people who witnessed their courage! Men and women of Tenochtitlan resisted! In tradition of our ancestors! May the resistance continue! May we never lay down our shields! May our hearts never weaken! May our minds remain in constant momentum with the collective actions of all of us!

2009

About the author:

Citlalli Citlalmina Anahuac is a student, activist, poet, and writer. She has been a proud member of the Mexica Movement (An Indigenous Rights Educational organization for the people of Nican Tlaca descent (Mexican, Central American, Native American, and South American) for the past 16 years. Anahuac's political/cultural awareness began in junior high school, when she witnessed the Prop 187 walk outs. She also started writing poetry in junior high thanks to the teachings of her English teacher who always encouraged Anahuac to express herself. In high school she joined the Mexica Movement and has been a community organizer working to get her people decolonized through protests, conferences, community universities, motivational speeches, and video production ever since. She is currently working on publishing other books to address the role of Nican Tlaca women (Mexican, Central American, and Native American women) in pre-1492 era to their role under the 521 year occupation. She graduated Cum Laude from East Los Angeles Community College 2013 with an emphasis on Behavioral Sciences and is planning to obtain her bachelors and masters in history. Ultimately she plans to teach History at junior colleges and help awaken others to knowledge of self and help build the self-esteem that our communities lack greatly. Meanwhile, she hopes to continue making videos and writing poetry that shed light on the hidden history of her people and continue combatting white supremacy racism in all aspects of life.

BIBLIOGRAPHY

If you would like to learn more on our history as Nican Tlaca (Indigenous) people, check out these books recommended by the Mexica Movement:

(Read in this order, please)
1 Daily Life of the Aztecs by Jacques Soustelle
2 Mexico by Michael Coe
3 Maya by Michael Coe
4 American Holocaust by David E. Stannard
5 Anahuac Book by Olin Tezcatlipoca located on this website
6 Colonizer's Model of the World by J.M. Blaut
7 American Indian Contributions to the World by Emory Dean Keoke & Kay Marie Porterfield

CHRONOLOGY AND OTHER REFERENCES:
8 Latin America: From Colonization To Globalization by Noam Chomsky
9 Encyclopedia of World History 6th Edition by Peter Stam
10 Oxford Atlas of History 2002 by Oxford Press
11 Course of Mexican History by Michael C. Meyer and William L. Sherman
12 Oxford History of Mexico 2000 by Michael Meyer and William Beezley
13 In the Language of Kings by Miguel Leon-Portilla
14 Skywatchers by Anthony F. Aveni
15 Flayed God (out of print, get used) by Roberta and Peter Markman

References:

Citlalli Citlalmina Anahuac youtube channel:

http://www.youtube.com/user/AnahuacWomenFight

Check out these other channels from other members and supporters of the Mexica Movement:

http://www.youtube.com/user/AnahuacPilgrimage

http://www.youtube.com/user/anahuacwarrior

Get informed. Get decolonized.

http://www.mexica-movement.org

CPSIA information can be obtained
at www.ICGtesting.com
Printed in the USA
FSOW03n0022201216
28748FS